S0-ASZ-397

FAMOUS FIGURES
OF ANCIENT TIMES

MOVABLE PAPER FIGURES TO CUT, COLOR, AND ASSEMBLE

CATHY DIEZ-LUCKIE

FIGURES IN MOTION
OAKLAND, CALIFORNIA

Copyright © 2009 Figures In Motion

All rights reserved. No part of this publication may be reproduced or transmitted in any form or by any means, electronic or mechanical, including photocopy, recording or any system, without prior permission in writing from the publisher. For information about permission to reproduce selections from this book, write to Figures In Motion, 6278 Clive Avenue, Oakland, CA 94611.

Published by:
Figures In Motion
6278 Clive Avenue
Oakland, CA 94611
(510) 482-8500
Email: info@figuresinmotion.com
Web: http://www.figuresinmotion.com

Visit **www.figuresinmotion.com** for additional information about upcoming titles in the *Famous Figures* series.

Printed in China.
ISBN 978-0-9818566-0-5

Publisher's Cataloging-in-Publication

    Diez-Luckie, Cathy.
        Famous figures of ancient times : movable paper
figures to cut, color, and assemble / Cathy Diez-Luckie.
        p. cm.
        SUMMARY: Provides brief descriptions of twenty influential people from ancient times, including Hammurabi, Moses, Nebuchadnezzar, Qin Shi Huangdi, Aristotle, Alexander the Great, Julius Caesar, Jesus, and others, along with drawings of each for children to cut out, color, and assemble. Drawings are based on authentic mosaics, paintings, and statues.
        Audience: Ages 6-12.
        ISBN-13: 978-0-9818566-0-5
        ISBN-10: 0-9818566-0-8

    1. Biography--To 500--Juvenile literature. 2. History, Ancient--Juvenile literature.
3. Toy and movable books--Specimens. [1. Biography--To 500. 2. History, Ancient.
3. Toy and movable books.]
    I. Title.

    D59.L83 2008   930
          QBI08-600210

This book is dedicated to my loving husband Jeff
who encouraged and supported me throughout the making of this book.

This book was created with love for my dear children Clarisse, Jesse, and Jeremy.

Thank you to my mother who inspired this book by telling me about how much fun
she had making 'fastener people' in school many years ago.

Stand at the crossroads and look;
Ask for the ancient paths,
Ask where the good way is, and walk in it,
And you will find rest for your souls.

Jeremiah 6:16

FIGURES IN MOTION CLUB

Join the Figures In Motion Club! Explore your love of history with our free quarterly e-newsletter.

In each issue you will receive:

Fascinating facts about the great men and women of history and the time in which they lived

Details about events and life in distant civilizations that make them come to life today

Links to explore famous people, archaeology, art, architecture, maps, geography, and more

Contests you can enter to win free prizes

Latest news on our upcoming titles

Visit **www.figuresinmotion.com** to join today—it's free!

Contents

WHAT THIS BOOK HAS TO OFFER YOU

For Children...

❧ Now you can make real moving figures of twenty of the most important people from thousands of years ago. Color your own costumes or use figures that have already been colored. Cut them out, put them together with fasteners, and make them move. You can also make them into puppets by attaching craft sticks or pipe cleaners to the moving figures.

❧ Have you ever wondered what advice Moses would give to Julius Caesar? What would Alexander the Great say to Emperor Qin Shi Huangdi, who built the Great Wall of China? Play out the real stories of history or make up your own and travel through time with moving figures!

For Parents, Educators, and Booksellers...

❧ *Famous Figures of Ancient Times* provides hands-on activities for children to study some of the people who shaped our world. Children love to use crayons, colored pencils, scissors and paper to create things. This book gives you a creative way to teach history by using activities that naturally appeal to them. Children will color, cut out and assemble figures that really move! Each figure has been printed on sturdy paper and may be assembled with mini brads, fasteners, or eyelets (p. 93).

❧ All of the illustrations in this book are true to period costume and where possible are based on authentic mosaics, paintings and statues. In addition to the black and white drawings, we've also provided pre-colored figures for children who would rather focus on the assembly and use of the figure. The back of each figure is labeled by name for easy identification after assembly.

❧ The *Famous Figures* series reinforces your child's history lessons and encourages them to study the great men and women of the past. Aristotle, Cyrus the Great, and Julius Caesar will come alive as children create their real moving figures. The book may be used independently or combined with any ancient history curriculum. The brief biographies we've included are only a start; students can follow the resource links on our website (Club link) to learn more about each person's life and the time period in which they lived. Plutarch, the ancient author of *The Lives of the Noble Grecians and Romans*, believed that we become better people through studying the lives of famous historical figures. This is one educational activity that is fun to make and play with!

For Museums and Historical Re-enactors...

❧ Inform and educate children about leaders from ancient Egyptian, Hebrew, Greek, Chinese, and Roman history as they visit your museum's collection or special exhibition. Let children take home a remembrance of what was experienced at your museum with *Famous Figures of Ancient Times*—while adding a revenue stream to your gift shop.

❧ The *Famous Figures* series is useful in generating interest for historical re-enactments. Costumes are meticulously drawn and historically accurate.

HOW TO MAKE A MOVING FIGURE

MATERIALS

Crayons, colored pencils, markers or paint

Scissors, ⅛" hole punch

Mini brads (⅛"), brass fasteners, or ⅛" eyelets (and setting tool)

PREPARE

◆ Remove the page of the figure that you would like to assemble from the book (tear at the perforation along the spine).

◆ Color the figure (skip this step for the pre-colored figures).

◆ Cut out each of the figure pieces.

◆ Make a hole for the fasteners by punching out each circular hole on the figure with a ⅛" hole punch.

◆ Place the figure pieces face down (back side up) so that the assembly letters and figure name are visible.

◆ Carefully match the letters together. **A Front** goes with **A Back**; **B Front** goes with **B Back**, etc.)

◆ Place the pieces marked **Front** under the pieces marked **Back** as you look at the back side of the figure. Place the pieces marked **Middle** in between the **Front** and **Back** pieces.

◆ Double check to make sure that all of the letters are matched together and that they are in the correct order. In some figures there may be up to four pieces that will be attached by one fastener. (i.e. Cyrus the Great)

◆ Note: For easier assembly, attach arms and legs together first before placing them on the body.

ASSEMBLE

Assembly with ⅛" mini brads or fasteners (no tool required)

◆ Insert the mini brad or fastener from the front side of the figure into the holes of the pieces to be joined together. The prongs of the brad or fastener should come out of the back side of the figure pieces.

◆ Separate the two prongs. Press them flat on the back side of the figure.

◆ Repeat the above until all of the holes are joined with brads or fasteners. The figure is assembled!

Assembly with ⅛" eyelets (setting tool required)

◆ Place the eyelet into the holes of the pieces to be joined together. Make sure that the back of the eyelet is coming out of the back/reverse side of the figure.

◆ Set the eyelet with an eyelet setting tool: a hammer, a hand held (silent) setter, or a table-top model eyelet setter, according to the manufacturer's instructions.

◆ Make the eyelet setting tighter if the figure pieces are too loose and swing too freely.

THE ANCIENTS

NARMER

It is believed that Narmer was the king who united Upper and Lower Egypt. Some historians believe he was also called Menes, a king from the 1st Dynasty.

The Narmer Palette (a large carved shield-shaped stone) shows a king who wore both the red crown of Lower Egypt and the white crown of Upper Egypt. The hieroglyphs on the palette name the king "Narmer." Narmer is holding a mace and a flail, two traditional symbols of Egyptian kingship.

King Narmer lived around 3150 to 3000 B.C.

KHUFU

Khufu was a pharaoh of the 4th Dynasty in Egypt. He is also known by his Greek name "Cheops."

The Great Pyramid, located in the plain of Giza, was built by Khufu and is believed to be his tomb. Thousands of people worked together for twenty years to build this magnificent structure. This pyramid is the largest of the original Seven Wonders of the Ancient World and is the only one that is still standing.

Snefru, also a pyramid builder, was the father of Khufu.

SARGON THE GREAT

Sargon of Akkad was also known as "Sargon the Great." He was the founder of the Dynasty of Akkad (Akkadian Empire) and reigned for 56 years. His family origin is unknown. In his younger days, Sargon was the cupbearer of the Sumerian King of Kish.
Sargon became a great military leader and conquered many cities in Sumeria and Mesopotamia. His empire was established in approximately 2334 B.C.
Sargon's greatest strengths were organizing and administering his vast empire. Most of what we know of Sargon came from legends and cuneiform history.

HAMMURABI

Hammurabi became the king of Babylon after the death of his father in approximately 1792 B.C. He strengthened and built up his own country and then went out and conquered neighboring regions.

He governed his land with a very detailed set of laws. Hammurabi's Code, found on a stone tablet over six feet tall, was one of the first written codes of law in history. Hammurabi was a strong leader who governed well and controlled his empire through the use of his laws.

MOSES

Moses was an Israelite baby hidden in a basket and found by the Pharaoh's daughter (date is uncertain). He was raised with royalty, but God called him to lead the Israelites out of Egypt. Moses became God's spokesman to the Egyptian Pharaoh and demonstrated God's power through many plagues God brought on the Egyptians. Moses received the Ten Commandments (a list of religious and moral commands given by God to be followed by the Israelites) on Mount Sinai. Moses led the Israelites through the desert on a journey to the land that God had promised to the Israelites.

KING DAVID

When he was a boy taking care of his father's sheep, David was anointed by the prophet Samuel to be king of Israel. God had withdrawn his favor from King Saul and decided that David would be king. David trusted God and was so courageous that he killed the giant Goliath with only his sling and some pebbles.

As king, David united the tribes of Israel into a mighty kingdom. He led his people by being a wise military leader, administrator, and diplomat. He was also a talented writer, composer, and musician. David was the father of King Solomon.

ASHURBANIPAL

Ashurbanipal was the last great king of ancient Assyria. He lived from 685 to 627 B.C. and was one of the few kings of his day who could read and write. He spent much of his reign in battle with neighboring lands.

Ashurbanipal was fond of stories and collected copies of all the clay tablets that were available (over 20,000) in the region and kept them in his palace at Nineveh. This collection of texts and documents formed the first library. Ashurbanipal believed that the library at Nineveh was the most important work he had accomplished as king.

NEBUCHADNEZZAR II

Nebuchadnezzar II was the ruler of Babylon in the Chaldean Dynasty around 605 to 562 B.C. He conducted many building projects in Babylon and built the Hanging Gardens of Babylon, one of the seven Wonders of the Ancient World. The gardens were described by several ancient Greek historians.

Nebuchadnezzar was known for his destruction of the temple in Jerusalem and his conquest of Judah, foretold by the prophet Jeremiah. Daniel was among the Jewish nobility taken to Babylon to serve King Nebuchadnezzar.

CYRUS THE GREAT

Cyrus the Great (also known as Cyrus II of Persia) founded the Persian Empire. He conquered the Median Empire, the Lydian Empire and the Neo-Babylonian Empire. Cyrus reigned from approximately 559 to 529 B.C.

Cyrus was successful because he made his newly conquered subjects into supporters. He was generous in promoting human rights and allowing freedom of religion, even if it was different from his own. Cyrus the Great allowed a remnant of Jewish captives to return from Babylon to Jerusalem to rebuild their temple.

A GREEK HOPLITE

The heavily armed citizen-warriors of ancient Greece were called hoplites. In battle, they were organized in a phalanx (row upon row of men in a rectangular formation).

The armor and weapons of each hoplite weighed about seventy pounds and consisted of: a helmet, a leather or bronze breastplate (cuirass) to protect the body, a shield (hoplon) which was like a wooden bowl that had bronze plates on the outside and leather on the inside, bronze greaves to protect the legs, a short sword with an iron blade that was carried in a scabbard, and a long spear.

ARISTOTLE

Aristotle was one of the most important Greek philosophers and founders of Western philosophy. He studied under Plato. Aristotle went to Macedon and became the tutor of Alexander the Great. Later he opened his own school in Athens called the Lyceum. Aristotle had many achievements. He invented the science of logic and wrote many important works about physics, ethics, politics, rhetoric, biology and zoology. Aristotle wanted to create order in government, so he described a system of monarchies, oligarchies, republics, and democracies. He created a method of sorting plants and animals into different groups.

ALEXANDER THE GREAT

Alexander became king when he was twenty years old. He was a brave young man and united into one region the city states of Greece that his father, Philip of Macedon, had conquered. Alexander was a great general. He gathered together a large army of Macedonians and Greeks and together they attacked the Persian Empire. Eventually, Alexander took over Turkey, Phoenicia, Egypt, and part of India.

Alexander died from an illness in Babylon in the palace of Nebuchadnezzar II when he was thirty-two years old.

Qin Shi Huangdi

Qin Shi Huangdi, the first Chinese emperor, had a powerful influence in China that lasted for over two thousand years. He united his country by standardizing money, weights, measures, and writing. The original Great Wall of China, built by Qin Shi Huangdi, was built of earth and required many men to build. Later the Ming Dynasty rebuilt the wall and made it stronger with bricks and stone. Emperor Qin ordered a gigantic army made out of terracotta (ceramic) to be buried with him in a large mausoleum. The army was life sized and had 8000 soldiers, 130 chariots and over 600 horses!

Hannibal

Hannibal was one of the world's greatest military commanders. He led the army of Carthage against the Roman army and won many victories over them.

Hannibal is best known for marching from Spain to Northern Italy, where he crossed the Alps with his army and war elephants (The Second Punic War, 218 to 201 B.C.). Eventually the Romans weakened his strong grip on their nation and Hannibal returned to Carthage. The Romans never forgot their fierce enemy and later conquered Carthage.

Hannibal's Elephant

Before Hannibal, Alexander the Great learned about the use of war elephants when they were used against him in a battle with the Persians. War elephants were first used in Europe by Carthage when they fought the Romans. Hannibal led 37 war elephants up over the mountains of the Pyrenees and the Alps and took the Romans completely by surprise. At first, the Roman legions were terrorized by the charging elephants. Eventually, the Romans learned how to handle the elephants by letting them go by, just as Alexander had done. After this, the elephants were no longer a threat to the Roman army.

Julius Caesar

Caesar was so successful in battle that he was given many honors. He conquered Gaul and invaded Britain for the first time. He also fought Pompey to rule Rome. Caesar was loved by the people and was chosen to serve in the Roman government. The senators resented Caesar's increasing power. When Julius Caesar was proclaimed dictator, several senators formed a plot to end Caesar's life and give the power back to the Senate. He died at their hands on March 15, 44 B.C. The people of Rome were outraged at the death of Caesar.

The month of July is named after Julius Caesar.

CAESAR AUGUSTUS

Octavian, whose name was later changed to Caesar Augustus, followed in his uncle Julius Caesar's footsteps in the leadership of Rome. He became the first Emperor of Rome and established a government that lasted for hundreds of years. Even though Augustus gave the Senate back all their power to rule the nation, he still had a tremendous influence in Rome. The rule of Augustus started an era of peace known as the Pax Romana, or Roman peace.

Augustus established Rome's first police and fire-fighting forces, improved the roads, and built a larger army. The month of August was named after him.

JESUS

Jesus was born in Judea in the first century. He taught about His Father, the kingdom of heaven, repentance, forgiveness, and eternal life. He taught people how they should live. There are accounts of Jesus healing many of the sick and even raising the dead.

The teachings and claims of Jesus angered some of the religious leaders in Jerusalem. He was crucified and died on a cross. Jesus later appeared to many of His followers. He said that those who made Him Lord of their lives and who asked forgiveness for their sins would be given eternal life.

CONSTANTINE

Constantine is best known for ending the persecution of Christians in the Roman Empire. He was the first Christian Roman Emperor. One story tells of Constantine seeing a vision on the day before the Battle of the Milvian Bridge. He saw a cross made of light with the words "In this sign you will conquer." The next day he fought under the protection of the Christian God and won the battle. Constantine issued the Edict of Milan in 313 A.D. This document made all religions legal throughout the entire Roman Empire. Constantine founded the beautiful city of Constantinople.

AUGUSTINE

Augustine was born in North Africa and spent much of his time reading and studying. In his younger days, Augustine chose to live a life that did not include God. His mother Monica prayed for him. He was excellent in rhetoric (the art of using words effectively in speaking and writing) and obtained a position at the imperial court in Milan. Augustine became a Christian and dedicated his life to God. He became a bishop and wrote over one hundred books. *The City of God* was written to defend Christianity, which was blamed for the destruction of Rome by the Visigoths in 410 A.D.

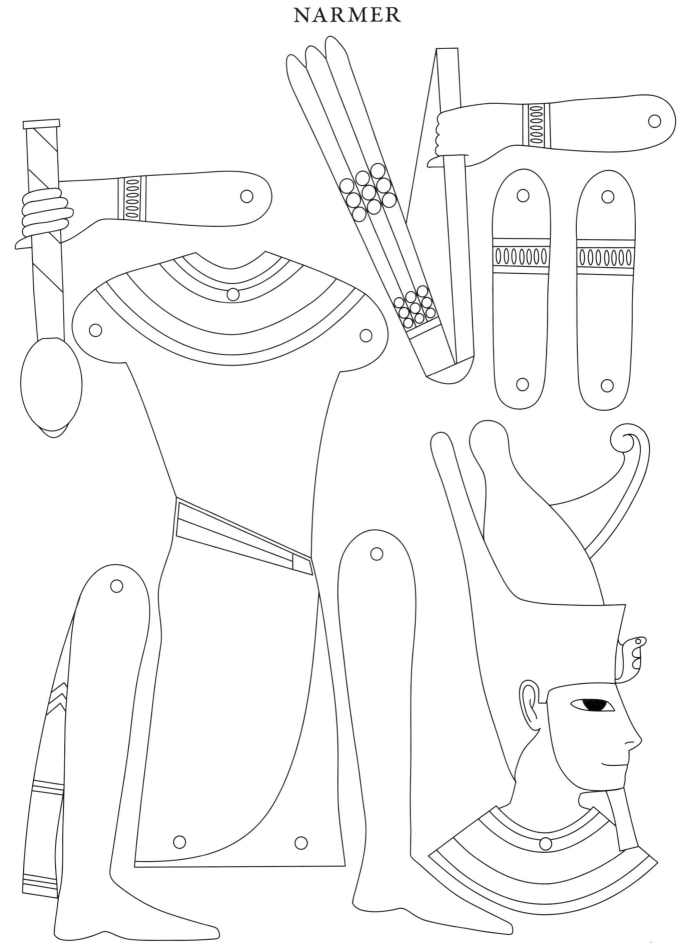

D
Front

B
Front

C
Front

G
Front

Back
G

Back
D

B
Back

A
Back

C
Back

**Narmer
Pharaoh of Egypt**

E
Back

F
Back

© Figures In Motion
www.figuresinmotion.com

Front
E

Front
F

A

Front

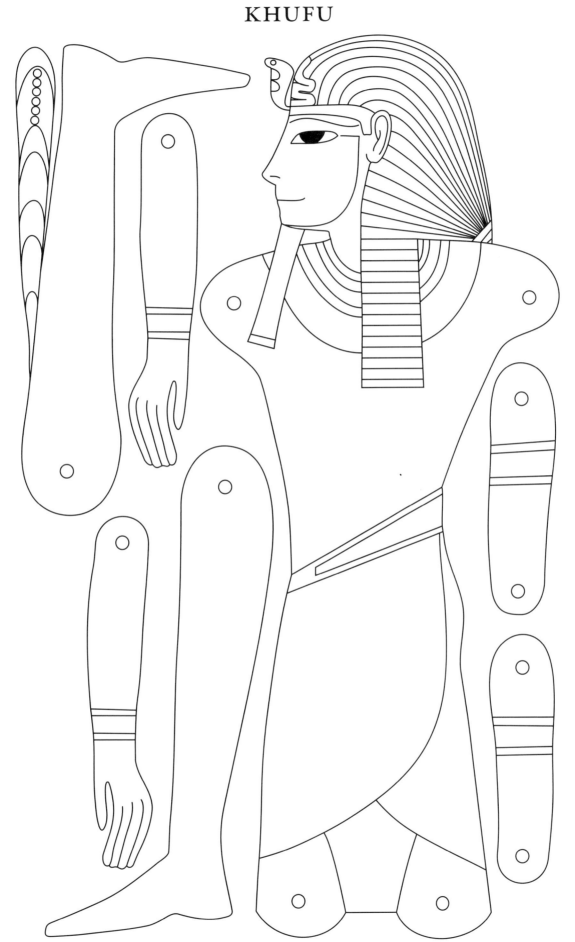

F
Back

A
Front

B
Front

Khufu
Pharaoh of Egypt

A
Back

C
Back

D
Back

© Figures In Motion
www.figuresinmotion.com

Front
E

E
Back

B
Back

Front
F

Front
C

Front
D

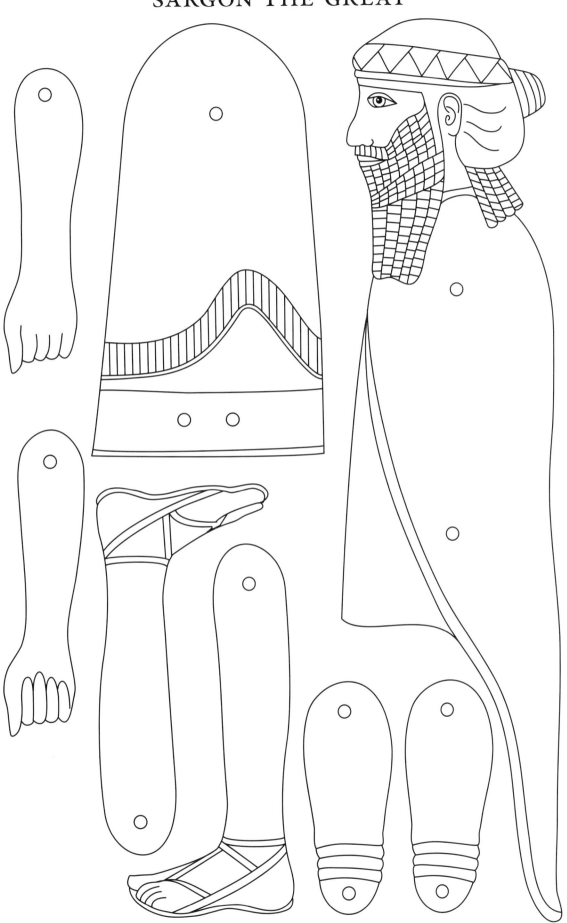

B

Back

C

Back

Middle
A

© Figures In Motion
www.figuresinmotion.com

Sargon the Great

Front Front
E **F**

D

Back

B

Front

E

Back

A **A**
Front Back

Back

F

Front Front
C **D**

HAMMURABI

C
Back

A
Back

Hammurabi

Back
D

A
Front

B
Back

© Figures In Motion
www.figuresinmotion.com

B
Front

C

Back
E

Front

Front
E

D Front

A
Back

B Front

B
Back

Moses

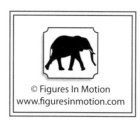

© Figures In Motion
www.figuresinmotion.com

C
Back

C

Front

D Front

A Front

D Back

A
Back

B Front

B
Back

Moses

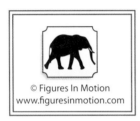

© Figures In Motion
www.figuresinmotion.com

C
Back

C

Front

D Front

A Front

D Back

KING DAVID

D
Back

B
Front

Front
D

B
Back

C
Back

King David

A
Back

© Figures In Motion
www.figuresinmotion.com

C
Front

A
Front

KING DAVID

D
Back

B
Front

Front
D

B
Back

C
Back

King David

A
Back

© Figures In Motion
www.figuresinmotion.com

C
Front

A
Front

B

Back

© Figures In Motion
www.figuresinmotion.com

C   **D**

Front   Front

E

Back

A

Front

C

Back

Front
E

A

Middle

Ashurbanipal

D

Back

B

Front

F

Back

F

Front

A

Back

B

Back

© Figures In Motion
www.figuresinmotion.com

C

Front

D

Front

E

Back

A

Front

C

Back

Front

E

A

Middle

Ashurbanipal

D

Back

B

Front

F

Back

F

Front

A

Back

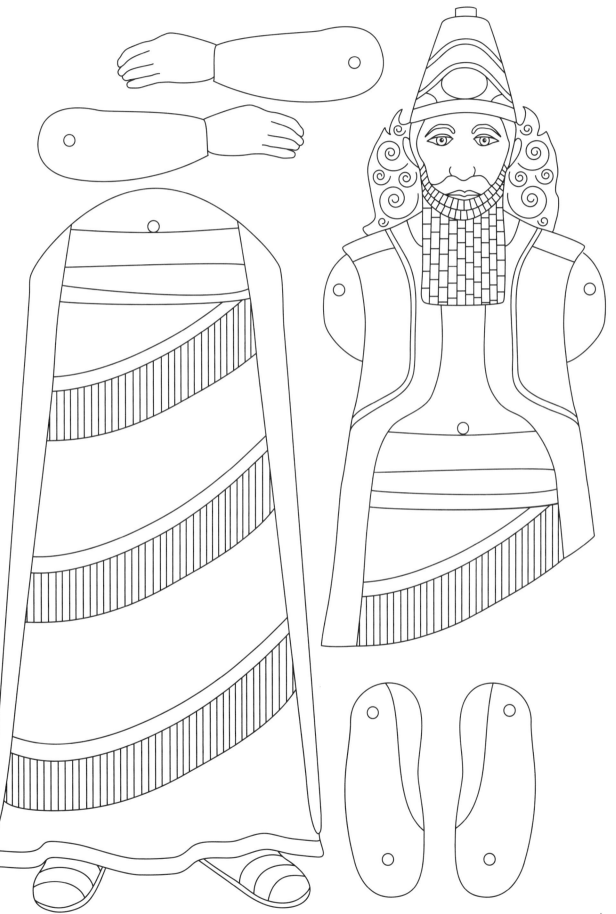

D
Front

E
Front

C
Back

A
Back

B
Back

Nebuchadnezzar II

C

Front

© Figures In Motion
www.figuresinmotion.com

A
Front

B
Front

Back
D

Back
E

CYRUS THE GREAT

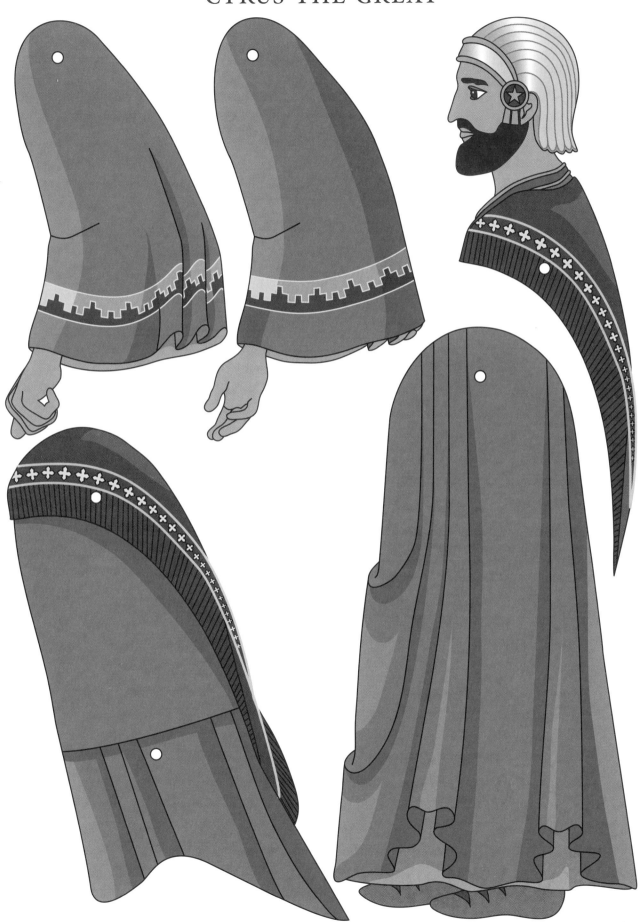

A
Back

A
Middle
Front

Front
A

B
Back

Cyrus the Great

© Figures In Motion
www.figuresinmotion.com

A
Middle
Back

B
Front

CYRUS THE GREAT

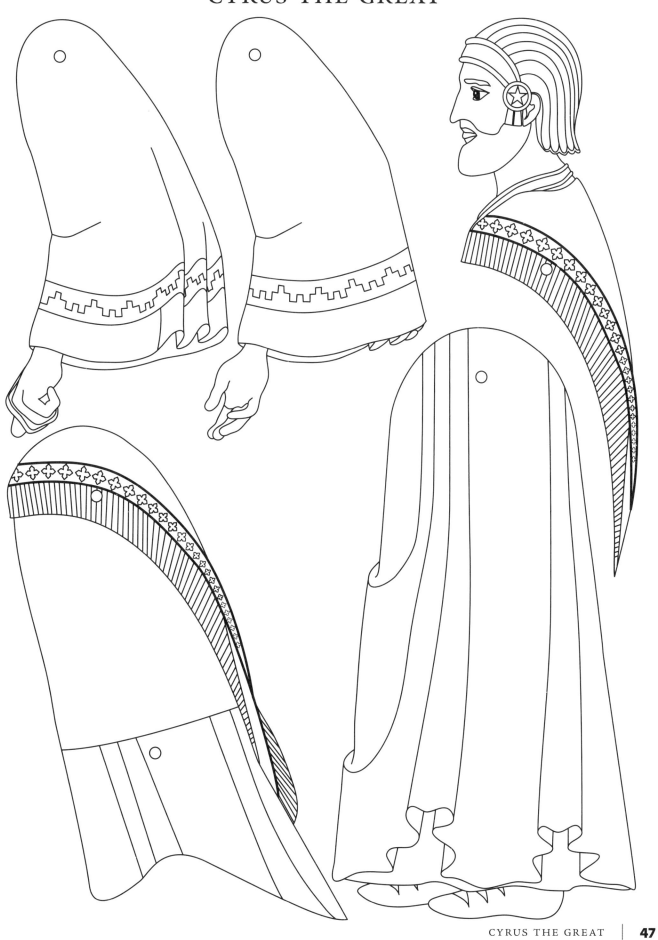

A
Back

A
Middle
Front

Front
A

B
Back

Cyrus the Great

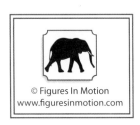

© Figures In Motion
www.figuresinmotion.com

A
Middle
Back

B
Front

A GREEK HOPLITE

C Back

A Front

C Front

A Back

A Middle

Greek Hoplite

© Figures In Motion
www.figuresinmotion.com

B Front

E Front

D Back

E Back

D Front

B Back

B Middle

QIN SHI HUANGDI

C
Back

Qin Shi Huangdi

© Figures In Motion
www.figuresinmotion.com

A
Back

B
Back

C
Front

A
Front

D
Front

B
Front

ARISTOTLE

B
Back

A
Back

D
Front

E
Front

A
Front

B
Front

Aristotle

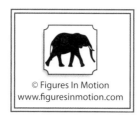

© Figures In Motion
www.figuresinmotion.com

C
Back

C
Front

D
Back

E
Back

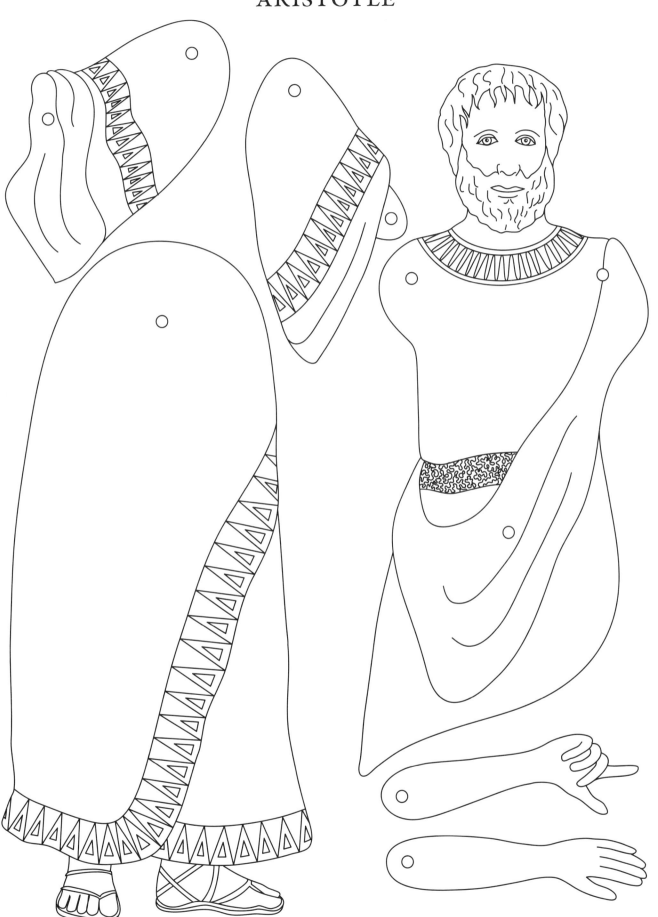

B
Back

A
Back

Front
D

Front
E

A
Front

B
Front

Aristotle

C
Back

© Figures In Motion
www.figuresinmotion.com

C
Front

D
Back

E
Back

ALEXANDER THE GREAT

C
Back

D
Back

A
Front

B
Front

Alexander
The Great

G
Back

E
Back

H
Back

F
Back

© Figures In Motion
www.figuresinmotion.com

Front
E

Front
F

G
Front

H
Front

A
Back

B
Back

Front
C

Front
D

HANNIBAL

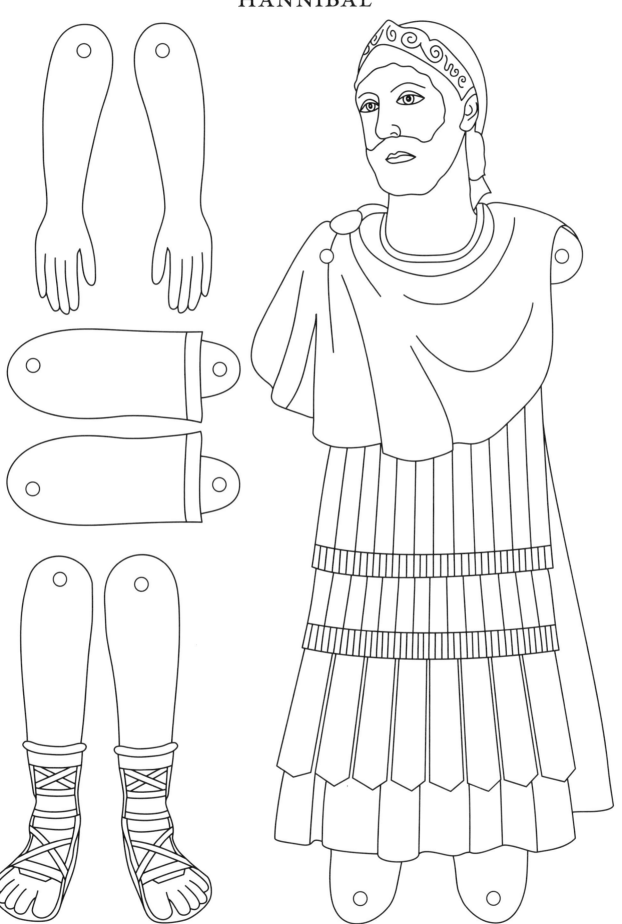

E
Back

F
Back

A
Front

B
Front

Hannibal

© Figures In Motion
www.figuresinmotion.com

E Front

A Back

F Front

B Back

C
Front

D
Front

Back
C

Back
D

C
Back

A
Back

C
Middle

B
Front

A
Front

Hannibal's Elephant

© Figures In Motion
www.figuresinmotion.com

B
Back

D
Front

C
Front

D
Back

D
Middle

JULIUS CAESAR

A
Back

D
Back

B
Front

C
Back

© Figures In Motion
www.figuresinmotion.com

A
Front

B
Back

Julius Caesar

C
Front

D
Front

JULIUS CAESAR

A
Back

D
Back

B
Front

C
Back

© Figures In Motion
www.figuresinmotion.com

A
Front

B
Back

Julius Caesar

C
Front

D
Front

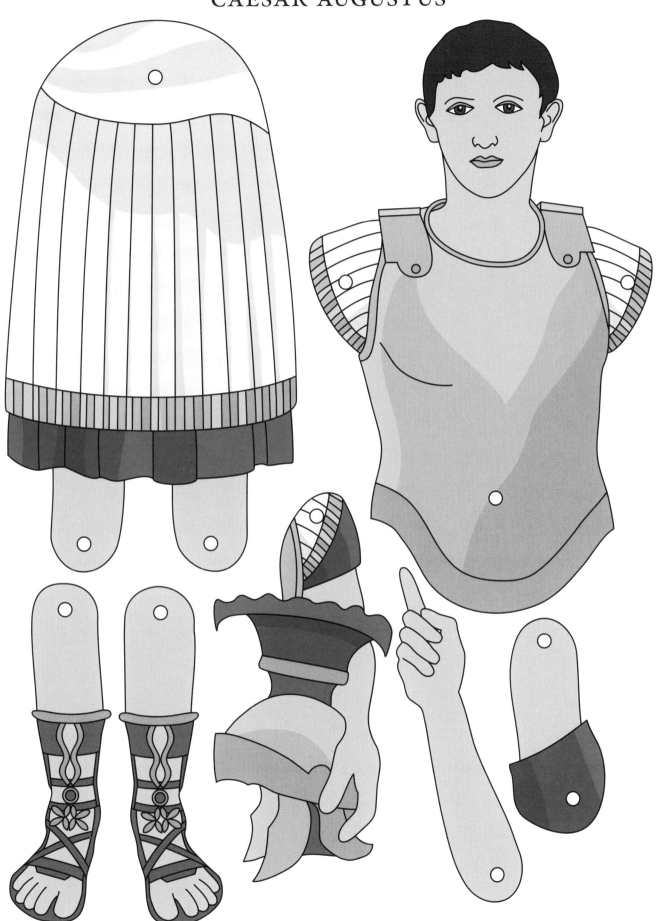

C

Back

A

Back

B

Front

Caesar Augustus

© Figures In Motion
www.figuresinmotion.com

C

Front

A

Front

Back

E

Back

F

E

Front

F

Front

D

Back

B

Back

D

Front

CAESAR AUGUSTUS

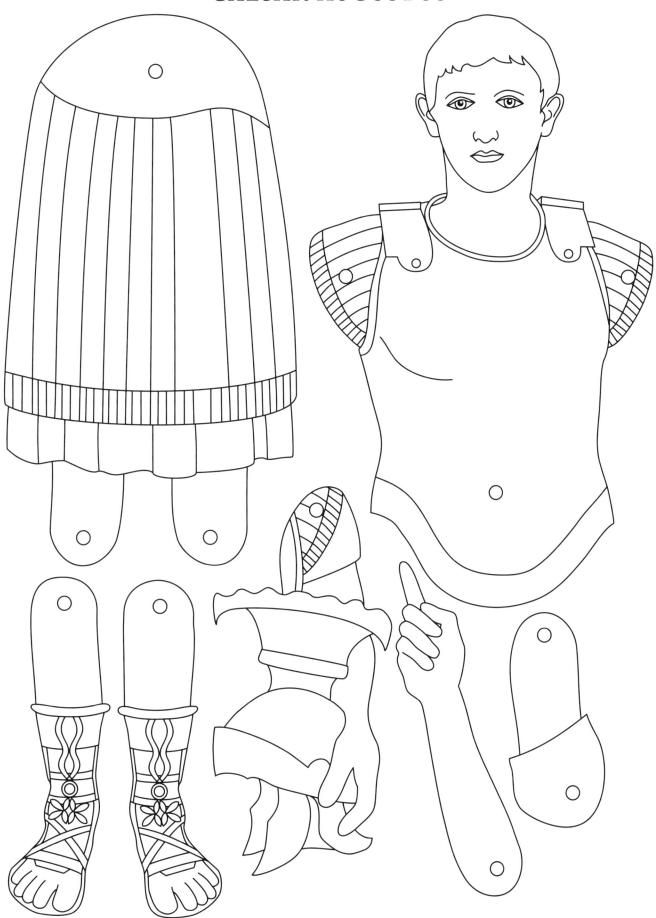

C

Back

A

Back

B

Front

Caesar Augustus

© Figures In Motion
www.figuresinmotion.com

C

Front

A

Front

Back

E

Back

F

E

Front

F

Front

D

Back

B

Back

D

Front

JESUS

A
Back

D
Front

D
Back

B
Front

A
Front

Jesus

C
Back

© Figures In Motion
www.figuresinmotion.com

C

Front

E
Front

B
Back

E
Back

CONSTANTINE

C
Back

A
Front

Front
C

A
Middle

Constantine

© Figures In Motion
www.figuresinmotion.com

D
Back

E
Back

F
Back

Front
B

A
Back

Front
D

Front
F

B
Back

Front
E

CONSTANTINE

C
Back

A
Front

Front
C

A
Middle

Constantine

© Figures In Motion
www.figuresinmotion.com

D
Back

E
Back

F
Back

Front
B

A
Back

Front
D

Front
F

B
Back

Front
E

C

Back

A
Front

B
Front

Ⅎ
Back

Augustine

© Figures In Motion
www.figuresinmotion.com

Ⅎ
Front

C

Front

B
Back

D
Back

D
Front

A
Back

RESOURCES

Figures In Motion Club

Join the Figures In Motion Club at www.figuresinmotion.com to explore your love of history with our free quarterly e-newsletter:

Learn fascinating facts about the great men and women of history and the time in which they lived.

Get details about events and life in distant civilizations that make them come to life today.

Explore links to famous people, archaeology, art, architecture, maps, geography and more.

Enter contests to win free prizes.

Receive the latest news on upcoming titles from Figures In Motion.

Hole Punch

The figures in this book have been designed to be used with a ⅛" round hole punch. Hole punches may be purchased from most local stationery or craft stores, or online at a variety of paper, craft or scrapbooking sites.

Fasteners

MINI BRADS (⅛") or BRASS FASTENERS — No tool required.

Round mini brads are ideal for assembling the moving figures. Simply punch the hole, insert the fastener, bend back the prongs of the fastener, and you're done. Mini brads do not require a special tool. Brass fasteners that are commonly sold in office supply stores may also be used to assemble the figures if their tips are short enough (the tip should be short enough so that it does not stick out past the edges of the paper when assembled). Mini brads may be purchased from most local craft or scrapbooking stores, or online at a number of paper, craft, or scrapbooking sites.

EYELETS (⅛") — Setting tool required.

Eyelets may also be used for assembling the moving figures but they require a setting tool. There are a variety of tools available on the market, from a simple hammer and punch set to a quiet and easy to use hand-held setting tool. Eyelets and eyelet setting tools may be purchased from most local craft or scrapbooking stores, or online at a number of paper, craft, or scrapbooking sites.

For more information on where to purchase any of the above items (hole punch, mini brads, fasteners, eyelets, and setting tools) please visit www.figuresinmotion.com.

ABOUT THE AUTHOR

Cathy Diez-Luckie

Cathy Diez-Luckie has illustrated several children's books, including *Goodbye Goose, Kitty Goes Splash,* and *The Paper Bag* (Richard C. Owen Publishers, Inc.). She is a nationally and internationally recognized airbrush artist. Her work has appeared in *The Encyclopedia of Airbrush Techniques, The Encyclopedia of Illustration Techniques,* World Trade Magazine, Stocks and Commodities Magazine, Via Magazine and other publications.

While Cathy's favorite artists include Hans Holbein, Johannes Vermeer, and Rembrandt, she has put away her paint and brushes for a digital pen and tablet to create the moving figures for this book.

In addition to her art training from the Toledo Museum of Art and the Academy of Art University in San Francisco, Cathy has a graduate degree in chemical engineering from Stanford University. She enjoys studying history, literature, science, and art with her children. Cathy and her husband Jeff home school their three children. The Diez-Luckies live in Oakland, California.

Famous Figures of Ancient Times has allowed her to combine her love of history and art together in a unique activity book for children. Cathy is working on a history series for Figures In Motion which will include *Famous Figures of Medieval Times, Famous Figures of the Renaissance, Famous Figures of the United States,* and *Famous Figures of the Bible.*

FIGURES IN MOTION
PUBLISHER OF CAPTIVATING ACTIVITY BOOKS
FOR CHILDREN

Discover the magic of history and the wonder of the past with children's activity books from Figures In Motion. These unique books make history come alive and allow children to explore their world and '*learn by playing*'. If you would like the latest information on book availability, please visit www.figuresinmotion.com/notify.

The *Famous Figures* Series Continues

Be the first to know as more of the Famous Figures series becomes available: *Famous Figures of Medieval Times, Famous Figures of the Renaissance, Famous Figures of the United States,* and *Famous Figures of the Bible*. Make moving action figures of the most recognized men and women of history. Act out the real stories of history or make up your own and travel through time with moving figures!

Moving Animal Fun from Figures In Motion

Do you like animals? How about dinosaurs and wild animals that move? You will have hours of fun making and playing with your moving animals from the upcoming books *DINOSAURS on the Move* and *ANIMALS Running Wild*!

www.figuresinmotion.com
6278 Clive Avenue   Oakland, CA 94611   510-482-8500

FIGURES IN MOTION

PUBLISHER OF CAPTIVATING
ACTIVITY BOOKS FOR CHILDREN

www.figuresinmotion.com

Coming soon from Figures In Motion...

Famous Figures of Medieval Times
Famous Figures of the Renaissance
Famous Figures of the United States
Famous Figures of the Bible

DINOSAURS on the Move
ANIMALS Running Wild

To find out when these books will be available,
please visit www.figuresinmotion.com/notify